Ankylosaurus

by Grace Hansen

DINOSAURS
Abdo
Kids

abdopublishing.com

Published by Abdo Kids, a division of ABDO, P.O. Box 398166, Minneapolis, Minnesota 55439.

Copyright © 2018 by Abdo Consulting Group, Inc. International copyrights reserved in all countries. No part of this book may be reproduced in any form without written permission from the publisher.

Printed in the United States of America, North Mankato, Minnesota.

052017

092017

 THIS BOOK CONTAINS RECYCLED MATERIALS

Photo Credits: Alamy, iStock, Science Source, Shutterstock, Thinkstock, ©edenpictures p.7 / CC-BY-2.0

Production Contributors: Teddy Borth, Jennie Forsberg, Grace Hansen

Design Contributors: Dorothy Toth, Laura Mitchell

Publisher's Cataloging in Publication Data

Names: Hansen, Grace, author.

Title: Ankylosaurus / by Grace Hansen.

Description: Minneapolis, Minnesota : Abdo Kids, 2018 | Series: Dinosaurs |
    Includes bibliographical references and index.

Identifiers: LCCN 2016962374 | ISBN 9781532100369 (lib. bdg.) |
    ISBN 9781532101052 (ebook) | ISBN 9781532101601 (Read-to-me ebook)

Subjects: LCSH: Ankylosaurus--Juvenile literature. | Dinosaurs--North America--
    Juvenile literature.

Classification: DDC 567.915--dc23

LC record available at http://lccn.loc.gov/2016962374

Table of Contents

Ankylosaurus

Ankylosaurus lived in the late **Cretaceous period**, around 70 million years ago. North America looked very different then. A shallow sea covered much of the land.

4

5

There were several

Ankylosaurus **species**.

But all had very similar

characteristics.

Habitat

Ankylosaurus lived in coastal areas. It was hot and humid. Many plants grew there.

9

Body

Ankylosaurus was a massive
dinosaur! It could weigh up
to 12,000 pounds (5,443 kg).
It was around 20 feet (6.1 m)
long and 6 feet (1.8 m) tall.

Ankylosaurus stood on four legs. Their bodies were tough and armored.

This dinosaur had a long and strong tail. It ended in a club. The club was probably used for defense.

Food

Ankylosaurus ate low-lying plants. They had leaf-shaped teeth and a beak. These worked well for plucking plants.

16

Fossils

The first Ankylosaurus fossils were found in 1900 in Wyoming. More have been found in Montana and Alberta, Canada. Footprints were found in Bolivia in 1996.

Montana

Wyoming

19

No full skeleton has been found yet. But two nearly complete ones have been uncovered. They have allowed us to learn about this awesome dinosaur!

More Facts

- Ankylosaurus means "fused lizard." This refers to the fused bones in its skull and other parts of its body.

- These dinosaurs were protected by bony plates, which probably helped them survive attacks.

- **Fossil** scientists, called paleontologists, believe that Ankylosaurus used their powerful tails to break the bones of other dinosaurs.

Glossary

armored – protected by a hard material.

characteristic – a certain feature that serves to identify a thing.

Cretaceous period – rocks from the Cretaceous period often show early insects and the first flowering plants. The end of the Cretaceous period, about 65 million years ago, brought the mass extinction of dinosaurs.

fossils – the remains, impression, or trace of something that lived long ago, as a skeleton, footprint, etc.

species – a group of animals that look alike, share many characteristics, and can produce young together.

Index

abdokids.com

Use this code to log on to abdokids.com and access crafts, games, videos and more!

Abdo Kids Code:

DAK0369